Cocoon
Water Child

VERONICA RED

The morning has finally come.

I will be watching a beautiful butterfly emerge from its old home.

It all began about a month ago.

A milestone from a tiny caterpillar to beautiful butterfly all on its own.

Caterpillar found a safe place to rest,
Attaching to a leaf that had been spun with
its silk thread.

Hidden inside, there is a wonderful change occurring.

First it must become soft and watery; it has everything needed to continue working.

Outside is a hardened case that has been protectively knitted,
Completely safe and supported and snuggly fitted.

It's a temporary house to protect against sunlight, winds, and small animals.
Like a mother's warmth, comfort and security are so valuable.

I have played soothing music every day to my future friend,

Communicating my happiness; a new phase
I am eagerly awaiting.

I want to let my friend know that even though it may feel confined,

I will be here to love and care for this move from deep within to the new outside.

The doorway is creeping open, making a choice to move now.

My heart is pounding, happy as it moves towards this path.

Here it comes, invited to greet the bright warm light,

Emerging from a period of sleep, from the wonders of the night.

Butterfly is revealed; wings are softly folded around itself.

Sleeping and getting some rest, all very important for its health.

This successful transformation has reached completion.

Hooray a new life, a brand-new beginning.

Growing and strengthening, gaining its brand-new energy,

It's happening quickly; my friend is getting ready to flee.

I feel so lucky to have watched this magic; it's been so liberating.

My gorgeous butterfly friend is slowing rising.

The new world is yours to explore and freely roam.

Fly away, take off, it's time to leave your throne.

Share your beautiful gifts and special talents. The world is ready for you to fully accept your elegance.

Veronica Red uniquely expresses her perspective relating to each element using her understanding of energies— earth, fire, air, and water—using astrology, tarot, and spiritual arts. Her fondness of each elemental energy was experienced in her childhood, giving her the loving passion to share with others a way to incorporate and celebrate the connection between our physical senses and our spiritual essences.

Her exposure in working with youth seeking support for mental health issues, along with her own children, revealed doubts in sense of self from an early age. She believes this to be of heavy past conditioning by society that encouraged huge changes in our natural templates rather than truly embracing our individual traits. Red's purpose in writing her stories is to shed light on the need to allow children to use their natural guidance and energies in a supportive environment that embraces them as a whole.

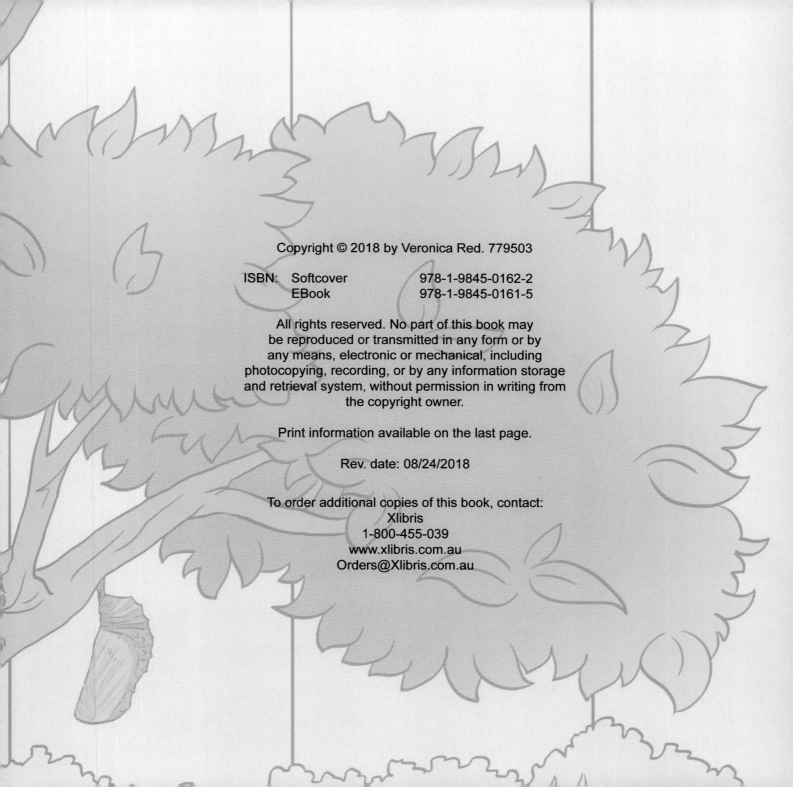

Print information available on the last page.

Rev. date: 08/24/2018

To order additional copies of this book, contact:
Xlibris
1-800-455-039
www.xlibris.com.au
Orders@Xlibris.com.au

Printed in the United States
By Bookmasters